The Power of a Woman

The Power of a Woman

poems

C. Steven Blue

The Power of a Woman

Published by Arrowcloud Press
Eugene, Oregon
Printed in the U.S.A.

First Edition

ISBN 10: 0-9635499-8-7
ISBN 13: 978-0-9635499-8-3

ARROWCLOUD
PRESS

For more information on C. Steven Blue
visit: www.wordsongs.com

TABLE OF CONTENTS

Silver Glistening Dreams

The Power of a Woman

Faraway Eyes

I would like to thank my wife, Paulette,
for her unwavering support.

I would like to thank my editor,
Katharine Valentino,
for her keen sense and understanding of my work.

I would like to thank my muse
for staying by my side
since I was a boy.

QUOTES:

Hillary Clinton:

Always aim high, work hard, and care deeply about what you believe in. And, when you stumble, keep faith. And, when you're knocked down, get right back up and never listen to anyone who says you can't or shouldn't go on.

Human rights are women's rights, and women's rights are human rights. Let us not forget that among those rights are the right to speak freely — and the right to be heard.

In this world and the world of tomorrow, we must go forward together or not at all.

Maya Angelou:

It's one of the greatest gifts you can give yourself, to forgive. Forgive everybody.

I think a hero is any person really intent on making this a better place for all people.

A bird doesn't sing because it has an answer; it sings because it has a song.

From the poem, "Phenomenal Woman":
Pretty women wonder where my secret lies. / I'm not cute or built to suit a fashion model's size / But when I start to tell them, / They think I'm telling lies. / I say, / It's in the reach of my arms, / The span of my hips, / The stride of my step, / The curl of my lips. / I'm a woman / Phenomenally. / Phenomenal woman, / That's me.

Silver Glistening Dreams

In This Catching

You look to me . . .
like somebody throwing up roses;
a prescient and perceptive human being.

You look to me . . .
like someone who doesn't do poses;
a peachy-skinned presence of fascination.

I catch . . .
your alluring demeanor,
the glow of your wondering gaze.

Your fervent, yet spare,
inclination to sing,
it shines through my wallowing haze.

I wonder what brings you to center,
to spring up and be
at this moment we're in.

I hope in this catching,
you'll let me slip up to
the magic that swallows your sin.

3/9/2015

Like A Wet Rainbow

Oh, to see the potential
of who you are inside,
like a flower—a carnation,
what a fragrance it could be.

To see the colors of you
sparkle, shine,
drip all over
like a wet rainbow,

the layers—the coats
could keep me warm
. . . forever

and could beat the hours of time
and the rustiness
out of my breath.

2/26/1990

Give Me Colors Galore

You are like . . .
An old familiar song
On the radio
One that soothes my soul

You are like . . .
A comet
Shooting through the sky
Out of control

Soothe my soul
Take me out of control

You are like . . .
The dewdrops
Kissing the grass
When you press your kiss upon my lips

You are like . . .
An open highway
Stretching out in front of me
On a long-awaited trip

Press your kiss upon my lips
Take me on a long-awaited trip

You are like . . .
A heater
Warming my heart
On a rainy day

You are like . . .
A lighthouse
In the fog
Showing a lost ship the way

Warm my heart
Show me the way

You make me feel like . . .
I'm touching the stars
And it's enough . . . But
You keep me wanting more

You are like . . .
A sunset
On the shore
With colors galore

Keep me wanting more
Give me colors galore

12/4/1989

The Archer

Slow and sure   Archer in the stars
Bended bow of elegance   you are
Subtle ways   penetrating gaze
           Thick, black, curly hair
Falling like grace   (on your shoulders)

Awesome Archer   bend your bow
Shoot your fresh flames   of desire
          Flame tips of longing
Sweet sting of passion   oil for my fire

         Stoned soul Goddess

         Perched on a pearl

In the presence   of your awesome womanhood
         Even the waves must curl

Caught in your glory   entwined in your magic
         Exquisite young girls swirl

The strength of your beauty   cannot be denied
All men are weak   from the times they have tried

Crumble me once more   into a limp repose
So soft . . . your neck   reveals your essence
       Musty syrup on a rose

I've always respected   the power of a woman
I've searched for the one   who might capture me

        And now . . .

The Archer bends her bow . . .

        Gloriously!

7/23/2013

7

Just Yesterday

For all the glory
and the faith
and all the time
I had to wait

For all the work
we had to do
for you to get to me
and me to you

God . . .
I feel tired
but elated
a strong appetite for kisses
but not hungry
for I feel . . . full
—fulfilled
from tip to toe

How was I to know
what you had in store

Just yesterday
I couldn't look lovers
in the eye
          yesterday
I couldn't listen
to their sigh
          yesterday
love songs made me want to cry
          just yesterday

But now you are here
and I feel alive again
with feelings I'd forgotten
growing stronger by the minute
          hour and day
and just yesterday . . .   feels so far away

8

Just yesterday
I knew that I would surely die
        yesterday
the tears welled up inside
        yesterday
springtime made me sigh
and yearn to roam like lovers do
        just yesterday

But today
the grass is greener
        sky is bluer
                love songs soar

Just yesterday
there was no one
but now . . .
there is so much more

Because now there is you

For all the glory
and the faith
and all the time
we had to wait

For all the work
we had to do
for you to get to me
and me to you

I am grateful
you are here
        today
and just yesterday . . .   seems so far away

4/3/1990

Strawberries

Since we've met
I've had this strong urge
to eat strawberries
  fresh
    nourishing
      effervescent

Each bite
soft on my lips
like your kisses
  sweet
    juicy
      succulent

Each kiss
a fragrant white petal
on a summer breeze
  floating softly
    in the air
      then landing

Each a small
but integral part
of a soft
  white
    fluffy
      featherbed

Each a unique
patch
in the quilt
  becoming
    our life
      together

One full of days
fresh for picking
strawberries
  you are
    still blossoming
      on the vine

4/20/1990

Slow Are The Days

When you're not at home
Sad that I miss you
This way
Like long ago
When I used to roam
Slow are the days

With all the shores
I've yet to comb
To feel this blue
I've got to say
Like the twilight I gloam
Slow are the days

The sky for me
Is monochrome
The moon has dues to pay
I shuffle
Through the sand alone
Slow are the days

Like sea waves
With cresting foam
That turn to invisible spray
It is as though
I fade away
Slow are the days

5/8/2010
—For Paulette

Lovely Bluesy Woman

She's a mean mistreater
But I love her
She's like an AC/DC heater
. . . Thinking of her

I love her truly
My love's unruly
When I'm with her
. . . I go crazy

My lovely bluesy woman
I'm a fool
She treats me cruel
. . . But I love her

10/30/1970

Love's Dry Rose

A single long-stemmed rose,
brought by you as an offering—a token,
a symbol of reconciliation,
still stands dried,
perfectly preserved
    in memory,
awaiting your return
from the misunderstanding
    silence
of your self-imposed isolation
from the love that was just learning
to share, express—caress
compassion, faith,
beginning to trust
    enough
that love could be trusted
to be there when needed
and it almost succeeded;
but time leaves love dry,
brittle, still, dusty—a memory
like the rose
and the nights without you,
still, silent, starless,
breaking the dawn
out there somewhere . . .
where you share this
beautiful morning,
this lonely
    mourning.

10/12/1991

14

Terry

Lemons on the tree
left there unpicked
rot in the rain
on *stormy Sunday.*

Well-worn flip-flops
still carry your tired feet
as you shuffle slowly through
your *no one to speak to* world.

Vague, infrequent memories
of making love; you would
rather just be touched
in all the aching places,

much kinder . . . and safer
than the risk of another
broken heart, long worn
like a thick terry robe

but without the comfort or warmth
or the ability to soak up
the wetness
of your lonely tears.

1/7/1995

15

Tempted By An Angel

Tempted by an angel
Speaking words of love
Tempted by an angel
A vision from above

She was the angel of your dreams
She was speaking the words of love
Tempted by an angel
Is all you were guilty of

You did the best you could
Worked hard to make things right
But no matter how hard you try
Some things just don't work out in this life

You paved the road to the *garden of Eden*
You even made her your wife
But in the end she left you
With nothing but guilt for the strife

Tempted by an angel
Speaking words of love
Tempted by an angel
A vision from above

She was the angel of your dreams
She was speaking the words of love
Tempted by an angel
Is all you were guilty of

You just can't seem to find someone
Willing to commit like you do
Yet you've still got your children . . . and your dreams
To carry you through

But you still see that sparkle that shines in her eyes
You still remember it all
And no matter how you try to ignore it . . . sometimes
You still hear the angel's call

Tempted by an angel
Speaking words of love
Tempted by an angel
A vision from above

She was the angel of your dreams
Speaking the words of love
Tempted by an angel
Is all you were guilty of

11/10/1998

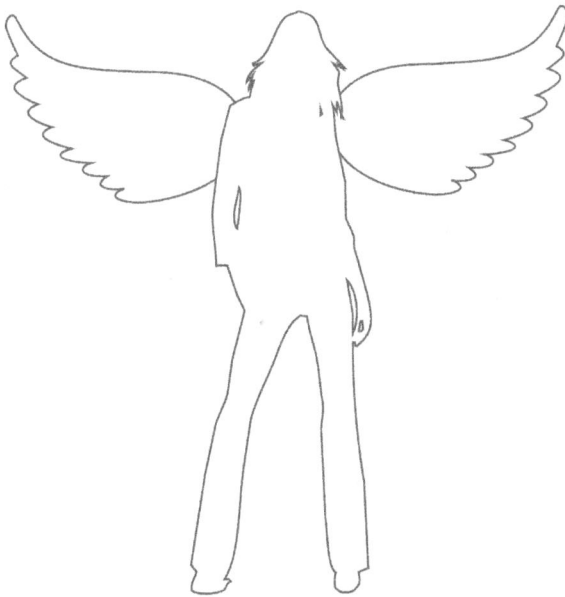

Timeless Love

In the fantasy reaches
Of our silver glistening dreams
Those moody metaphors
Still reach out . . .
To touch our memories
And unite the streaming consciousness

Although the words we never said
May haunt us for all time
I'll not regret we ever met
I loved you in my prime

This song that now comes sentient
Reminds me of those years
The thrill of love . . . the sadness
And even the lonely tears

Although I can't replace them
They'll live on in this song
We'll always be reminded
Of a timeless love so strong

In the fantasy reaches
Of my silver glistening dreams
These moody metaphors
Reach out to touch our memories
And unite the streaming consciousness
        Once more

12/25/2011

The Power of a Woman

Live For Me

I made the mistake of a lifetime
When I sold my Sunshine's soul
I couldn't help it
I wanted so much
What I never could control

Mama's gonna mold Sunshine
Into a money-making machine
      To be what she
      Could never be
A beautiful glamour queen

She's sold her little Sunshine
To the feast-or-famine play
It's not for the money
But just for love
Is what she'll always say

Now she slides onto the pillow
To steal another man
To make her feel
The way she wants
Anyway she can

To stuff the guilt built up so long
She cannot bear to face
But if he don't help
She'll find some drinks
And a man in another place

I made the mistake of a lifetime
When I sold my Sunshine's soul
I couldn't help it
I wanted so much
What I never could control

But Sunshine doesn't understand
She's too young to know what it means
        To sell herself
        As a beauty queen
With all the other money machines

She doesn't like the spotlight
        The makeup
        Or the curls
She doesn't feel she's made up like
The other glamour girls

She just wants to have some fun
Like other little girls do
But Mama is strong
And just doesn't see
What she's putting Sunshine through

She's just another contestant
Too young to speak up for her dream
Too young to protect herself
        From the predators
Who make her insides scream

. . . And Mama's best intentions
. . . Are never what they seem

I made the mistake of a lifetime
When I sold my Sunshine's soul
I couldn't help it
I wanted so much
What I never could control

Oh Sunshine . . .
You're a poor girl
Mama always likes to say
But I'm gonna make you famous
And you'll be a star someday

Then everyone will look at you
And see the beauty I see
We'll be so rich
I'll never worry no more
What people think about me

What a life we're gonna have
What a world it's gonna be
Nothing's gonna stop us now
We'll be so happy
. . . You'll see

If you'll only
    Just
        Live for me

I made the mistake of a lifetime
When I sold my Sunshine's soul
I couldn't help it
I wanted so much
What I never could control

1/29/2011

Dunnigan Falls Meth Lab Lair

She was a poor but comely girl
Grown up on a podunk road
Abused by those who should help
—Having to carry that heavy load

It took away her power
The only strength a young girl has
The power of a good woman
. . . Now gone bad

It took her too many places
She never wanted to be
Using her body to gain some leverage
Was the only way she could see

She wanted to move forward from the hard times
She wanted to strike out on her own
She wanted to forget all the abuse and corruption
            But she was all alone

She'll never forget
How it all went down
How he wooed her and spoiled her
All over town

Then he hit her and beat her
Till she couldn't see clear
Let him do what he wanted
As she gave in to fear

She'll never forget
Why he took her there
To the Dunnigan Falls
Meth lab lair

Subjecting her
. . . A troubled girl
To the sullied world
That existed there

He caught her in the moment
She was weakest . . . at best
She'd escaped from the worst
And disregarded the rest

He saw that she was hungry
Took advantage 'cause he could
He'd done it so many times before
He was just no fuckin' good

He couldn't remember a time
When he'd ever had any regrets
About using a young girl's body
To get whatever he could get

He took her to the meth lab
Traded her for a score
Let them use her and abuse her
Till he got what he wanted . . . and more

He left her there . . . forsaken
With nothin' but her shame
And went off lookin' for the next young girl
Another victim to claim

She'll never forget
Why he took her there
To the Dunnigan Falls
Meth lab lair

Subjecting her
. . . A forgotten girl
To the sullied world
That existed there

She escaped eventually
Got away for good
Headed down south
As far as she could

She wanted revenge
But didn't dare try
All she could do
Was lay down and cry

Then she pulled herself up
Like it always had been
She was a good girl gone bad
Tryin' to be good again

So many years now
Workin' hard as she can
And it's still damn hard
For her to trust any man

But if one comes along
He'd best be in no hurry
As the struggles of her past
Still cause her eyes to get blurry

He'll never know the life she had
Or what she had to do
Unless he proves his virtue first
He'll never know what she's been through

'Cause . . .
She never can forget
Why he took her there
To the Dunnigan Falls
Meth lab lair

Subjecting her
. . . An innocent girl
To the sullied world
That existed there

She'll never forget
Why he took her there
To the Dunnigan Falls
Meth lab madness

Subjecting her
. . . An innocent girl
To that sullied world
And all its sadness

10/27/2017

The Power Of A Woman - #3

For you and me
It's a time of trouble
Feast or famine
Wherever we go

It may sound simple
. . . Yes it's true
But help one another
Is what you've got to do

That's still it
Don't you know
The second coming
Will show

The second coming
Will be a woman
Nurturing and compassion
Is what will show

—It's got to be
Don't you know
It's what we need . . . now
To grow

      Higher . . . spiritually

Can't you see
All the waste we make
In our haste

We leave behind
So much trash
To get there too fast

But where is it
We are going
Do you think you know

You may think
You're growing now
But the second coming
Will show

The second coming
Will be a woman
Nurturing and compassion
Is what will show

—It's got to be
Don't you know
It's what we need . . . now
To grow

Higher . . . spiritually

Goddess of Love
Brings the Light
To shine on our needs

Coming soon
To a state of mind
Near you

10/17/1991

29

The Power Of A Woman - #5

Some things are bigger than you!
If you are in contempt
and not in support,
you will be on the wrong side
        of history.

This is the time of women,
the time of woman power,
the time to evolve beyond the limits
of the patriarchal society
we all grew up in;
the one that has driven the world for so long;
the one that has driven us to the brink
of perpetual war and annihilation.

But we have a history of diversity,
        human rights
and the struggle for equality,
which has brought us to this moment.
A paradigm shift is upon us!

If you are not in support,
you are on the wrong side of history.
Not the written history
put down by the dominant influences
of power, taken up after conquering
        or a coup,
but the history of this moment
in our evolution.

Be on the right side of history.
Be on the side moving forward.
It is truly a matter of light or dark.
If you look into your heart,

the choice cannot be more clear.

8/1/2016

Poetry—The Ballerina

1.
An aged tree
struggles to grow free from itself,
its outer branches turned inward,
twisting, turning, pushing in and up
then outward again
throughout the years
as it struggles through life
—a countless calendar
for all intents and purposes,
an elegy of our inhumanity to nature,
if it could speak.

The prima ballerina . . . retires!

2.
Structured steel
struggling to be free from itself,
its countless cables of iron twisting
across, downward, around each other
then upward again.
Giant steel beams pinnacle
as if struggling for life
—a welded calendar.
Dedication of humanity,
an ode to science and entertainment
is what it seeks.

The prima ballerina . . . is born!

3.
Poetry . . .
you are the ballerina.
The song of your dance
takes wings in my heart
—it soars.
It flies inside me
but you are also the swan.

Poetry . . .
like flowing verse,
your rhythm.
Your movements
melt together
like snowflakes
in the sun.

Twirl me into a trance.
Take all of me
into your dance.
No feather . . . no down!
Your passion is poetry.
    You are
the ballerina.

8/17/1990
—For Nina Ananiashvili
(No feather . . . no down
is the Russian term for
break a leg)

Song For My Mother (excerpt 1)

It's not that we're different
      How can it be
It's just that we care more now
      Can't you see

If the feeling is real
Then it's one to believe
That we all can perceive
What is real
If we feel it's our way
Then we'll make it someday

And it's here
      It's right now
            I must show you
. . . But how
You must pick up on something
Much closer right now

. . . Just to see you
. . . Just to be with you
If you know this feeling
Then it all will work out

I just want you together
We all must come now
Yes, where love sticks together
It's here and here's how
It will stand as it stood
But the love's deeper now
And I don't even know
If the time is right now
But it's just that I'm feeling
. . . So feeling
. . . Somehow

6/26/1970
—For Mom

34

In The Absence Of You

Mom used to tell me I was the one
who always brought home the stray dogs,
not my brother, not my sister, but me.
Frightened, were they drawn to me or I to them?
Their rescue protected my serenity.

I continue to rescue,
but now people, it seems,
often to the detriment
of my well being.
What part of the inner me
do I attempt to liberate each time?
Is my psyche so shackled?
Will a stray restore my freedom
. . . or add to my angst?

Maybe I'm trying to piece back together
that which I have lost.
If I can fix you, then maybe
you will fix me.
But it never works
and the cost is my serenity.

Perhaps I need to accept
that compassion and empathy
are only pieces of life's puzzle
and do not always bring serenity
in the complex maze
of the universe.

It's hard to tell
what now I do,
to try to get through
in the absence of you.

In those final years of Alzheimer's,
when I was able to care for you,
I recalled how you always rescued me.
I was able to be there for you,
maybe not to rescue,
but to just see you, be with you.

And, even almost to the end,
when I would play for you
the music you loved
—your music, the music you grew up with—
it would always reach you.
I could see it in your eyes
. . . and you would smile
. . . and we would dance.
There was still that recognizable spark!

And I continue to rescue . . .
But now it is me, it seems,
to the eternal harmony
of my well being.
It's easier to tell
what now I do . . .
as a blossoming tear
            breaks through
                        in the absence of you.

Thank you, Mom,
for letting me bring home
the stray dogs.

5/6/2008
—For Mom

Try To Remember You

Why were you here
Why did you have us
Why did you try so hard
Yet sacrifice your own happiness

I think of you
When times are hard
Your heart was in the right place
Though sometimes I did not understand

It's a hard world to survive in
It's a tough one, yes it's true
But it always gives me comfort
When I think of you

You brought music into my life
Made me feel happy about it
Watching you dance was always
—Always . . . magical

When a funky beat moves me now
Saves me from feeling blue
When it's hard to cope in this troubling world
Sometimes I just think of you
. . . Try to remember you

You sacrificed your whole life for us
I wonder what you really wanted
I know you had eight years
Of real happiness
With your one true love

But it doesn't seem like much
To trade
For a life of hard labor
Little rewards to show
For memories lost
And life so restricted

You seemed to be content
With what little you had found
And you always made me glad
That you were mine

You were always the one
To pick me up
Dust me off
And help me move on

You could always carry me through
        It's true
                And I miss you so

I think of you
When times are hard
Your heart was in the right place
Though, sometimes I still . . .
Do not understand

12/23/1997 & 4/30/2010
—For Mom

By Your Side

When you were so small
I could still hold you in my arms,
I used to sing you to sleep at night.
Your eyes would light up
when I came into your room.
     I could tell
you always wanted me by your side.

As you grew older
and went off to school,
I couldn't always be there
to comfort or protect you.
But when I would see you,
my heart-felt voice was there
with reassurance.
You'd hug me, smile,
     and I knew
you always wanted me by your side.

And now you've grown so fast
into womanhood.
Sometimes we've lived together
but now you're on your own again.
We've seen how hard life can be,
but it's made us each stronger
in our own ways.
No matter what you do or where you go,
there's one thing I want to make sure
     you know,
I'll always be there by your side.

In the future as a woman,
with a life and family of your own,
I know you'll be strong, proud and caring,
because you are sensitive
and make good decisions.
Through the pain and joy of your life
I want you to remember
        and realize
I'll always be there by your side.

And someday . . .
you might be singing a song
to your own son or daughter
at bedtime,
and their eyes might light up
like yours did.
If you do, I hope you are reminded
        of us,
and I hope you will remember
        what we know . . .
I'll always be there by your side.

1/31/1990
—For Tara

41

Through The Eyes Of A Child

I can see once again
Through the eyes of a child
As I remember a little one
Who loved to run wild

On Easter Morning
So anxious for the egg hunt
In your brand new dress
So full of excitement

I can still see that little girl
The glow of wonder in her eyes
Who showed exuberant love
Through her giggles and her sighs

Now it's hard to realize
How quickly you have grown
To proud and glorious womanhood
Carrying a child of your own

A child you've wanted dearly
You've tried for so many years
A child you thought you'd never see
You fought back so many tears

I'm grateful now and filled with joy
Your time is finally here
I'll love him like I've loved you
As you enter this new frontier

You know I'm proud as a father can be
To see you excited again
Just like those days when you were young
So eager for your life to begin

Through the eyes of a child, I know you'll see
The joy your little boy can bring
When it's your turn, in his growing years
To share his joy and sing

Just as I'm still singing to you
In my heart where it always is true
That you're still my little girl running wild
I can see again . . . through the eyes of a child

4/2/2010
—For Tara

Faraway Eyes

The Look In Your Thunder

How many times in my life can I say
I saw that look in your eyes
      From far away
You saw me too
Our glances locked
But it was never meant to be

And always . . . I wondered what if . . . what if you . . .
What if you hadn't stepped onto that train
What if I wasn't stuck in the rain
What if we had met for real
Over the vast terrain of this lifetime

I caught your gaze
But didn't get to keep it
—Gone with my fumbling blunder
Left here on my own . . . all alone again
Down under the look in your thunder

Were you dazzled as well
By the vibrations we swapped
What was the power you had over me
Could it be the allure of an unspoken love
Now gone with the waves into eternity

Or was it just . . . melancholy thoughts
Caught in the moment of a chance encounter
What if it wasn't what I thought I saw
And what if you never saw it at all
—But I saw it . . . I know I saw it

The look of your gaze
I didn't get to keep it
—Gone with my fumbling blunder
Left here on my own . . . all alone again
Down under the look in your thunder

9/02/2017

Sparkling Wonder

I gaze at you
From across the room
I wonder what it is
Drawing me to you

I can see in your eyes
You feel it too
Every time you have a chance
You glance at me

You are striking
In my eyes
But you could be my demise
Shall I play the fool again

Dark-haired beauty
With long flowing curls
Speak to me
With grace and glory

I yearn to know
The story in your eyes
If you could warm me
With your surprise

I can see you shimmer there
Are you aware of how I feel
Do you really feel it too
—Could you . . . would you

Tell me sparkling wonder
What is it makes you shine
Why am I drawn to you
Wanting you . . . to want me.

1/21/2012

Love's Prose

Out of thin air you appeared
I saw you from across the room
Our eyes fixed on each other
      Like magnets
A breeze drew me to your perfume

You strolled towards me with purpose
Your smile lit up the whole place
You seemed to see me
The way I saw you
It was written all over your face

Come to me
My blooming rose
Carry me away
      I propose
Sing me your beauty
In soft-spoken words
Teach me the way of love's prose

Out of thin air we created
A love that was destined to be
It happened so quick
In a time freeze
The waves of love crashed on the sea

I brought you out of slow yearning
To heightened flames of desire
You lit me so hot
I burned on the spot
And nothing could put out the fire

Come to me
My blooming rose
Carry me away
        I propose
Sing me your beauty
In soft-spoken words
Teach me the way of love's prose

10/14/2010
—For Paulette

Smoulder In Your Gaze

The longed-for love song
of winter's brazen chill
is there when I gaze
at firelight in your eyes

Embracing my mere thoughts
        you see
that which I only imagine
belonging to that magical realm
caught between thoughts
and embraces

In the traces of your lilting
        fingers
warm on the scruff of my neck
I melt into summer getaways
no longer nipped
by winter's brittle freeze

I see the reflection
of love's passioned moments
. . . the smoulder in your gaze
of what is yet to come
        blanket bliss
and embered lips
pressing all our winter worries
        away

7/25/2011
—For Paulette

Away

Languishing beauty
of love's lost refrain, searching
my heart to follow
the feeling of empty dreams.

In the gathering storm
I sense the fading sunrise,
whose gleam now drips . . .
A ship sails away in the night.

Never shall the time seem slower
nor grow the heartache
deeper. From this dream
I cannot awaken.

Retrieve what is left of happiness
—run fast to catch a glimpse
before it crosses the horizon
of emptiness.

Oh, how I long for . . .
that which cannot be followed,
how I reach for . . .
that which cannot be touched,

how I yearn for . . .
that which my heartbeat remembers
—what is gone forever.
I must move on,

but all I can see
is the future that cannot be,
as I awaken to you softly . . .
kissing those memories
away . . .

3/8/2011
—For Paulette (upon awakening from a nightmare)

51

Even In My Dreams

Beautiful music
  Was made just for you
    You sleep like an innocent child

I like to call you my girl . . . but
  There's something inside you
    Seems a bit wild

The wave of your hair . . . like the curl
  On the waves of the sea
    I love the way you gaze at me

The inquisitive blink of your lashes
  Reminds me of
    the Cheshire Cat

I ponder the roundness . . . of your body
  You giggle with dimples
    I like you like that

Your eyes are so clear
  They sparkle
    Like starlight

You're warm when we mingle
  You hold me
    So tight

You're sweet and supple
  Like a nineteen year old bronze beauty
    You're even in my dreams

I yearn for your calling
  That swelter
    You've got

I drip when you love me
Your feelings
So hot

We are honest
With each other
My heart feels strong

We hold hands
When we sleep
We meld for so long

I feel like we
Belong together
I love the way you moan

You even do that
In my dreams
How quickly we have grown

How innocent you seem
Asleep
Curled up in a ball

The secret I keep
. . . Is
I love it all

You're sweet and supple
Like a nineteen year old bronze beauty
You're even in my dreams

You're sweet and supple
Like a nineteen year old bronze beauty
You're even in my dreams

2/28/1988

53

The Window Where You Look

Tiny as the seeds of rain
Lush and green the vast terrain
A deep ocean sky foggy smeared
High above the clouds have cleared

Pigtails prance so near me now
Green carpet coats the lover
Different colored smiles allow
Much to be uncovered

So near and yet untouchable
To read you like a book . . .
Which needs its pages slowly turned
To the window where you look

Vast the shroud, like spilled whipped cream
Conjures up your colored dream
Into something showable
Is your magic knowable

Mount in dream time proud and private
Brave your knowledge and describe it
Graded in a lower score
I would have you give up more

Leather lounging shook me up
Drenched me in your buttercup
Captured colors braided close
Leave me with an overdose

Double cover, softened layers
Signify the lustful players
Mounds of luscious hand-clasped moans
Draw me to your stranger zones

As we languish between shaking sleep
And rumbling awake
The sky curls
Like layers on a lake

Or clothes
On a newly bloomed rose
Your sigh is the reason
I suppose

Open the cabinet
Discover your stash
Sprinkle with rose water
In a hot flash

Fun on a dime
Just in time to discover
It's easy, you know
Because . . . you're my lover

Snow-capped silhouettes
Linger below
Melt in a moment
From the view of your glow

How can we linger now
When we drop down
For dream time is over
And we've touched the ground

11/12/2010
—Dream poem written upon awakening
from a nap on an airplane

Find Yourself

It's hard sometimes
Letting you go
I was looking for a full-time love
Didn't you know?
    And you were looking
    To find yourself

But it's always fun
Watching you grow
Observing self-discovery
Makes my insides glow (Does it show?)
    While you're just looking
    To find yourself

So go on flower
. . . Bloom!
I'll just dance around my room
And tingle inside for the knowing
    Go on flower
    . . . Bloom!

It's awkward sometimes
When you call
And I have nothing to say at all
Because I know
    You're still looking
    To find yourself

There's so much
I'd really like to say
But it all stems from yesterday
So I let it go
    And watch you
    Looking to find yourself

So go on flower
. . . Bloom!
I'll just dance around my room
And tingle inside for the knowing
        Go on flower
            . . . Bloom!

6/14/1991

The Power of a Woman

. . . The End

APPENDIX

CREDITS

Cover design: Steven C. Schreiner
Manuscript design/layout: Steven C. Schreiner
Graphics design: Steven C. Schreiner
Editor: Katharine Valentino
Proofreaders: Paulette Schreiner, Michele Graf, Charles Castle

Thanks to my critique group for helping me tweak and polish the final drafts of some of the poems in this book

PERSONAL PHOTOS/GRAPHICS

—Front cover photo: Steven's daughter, Tara Schreiner Steele
—Page 1 photo: Steven's wife, Paulette Schreiner
—Page 37 photo: Steven's mother, Phyllis Schreiner Brown
—Page 43 photo: Steven's daughter, Tara Schreiner Steele
—Page 45 photo: Steven's mother, Phyllis Schreiner Brown
—Page 65 photo: C. Steven Blue

All photos are from the Steven C. Schreiner collection.
All photographic re-design and manipulation by Steven C. Schreiner

OTHER PHOTOS/GRAPHICS

—Back cover graphic: Pixabay.com,
re-design and manipulation by Steven C. Schreiner
—Page III: original graphic: Vecteezy.com,
re-design and manipulation by Steven C. Schreiner
—Page 2: original graphics: weheartit.com/123649425 -
fernanda; depositphotos.com/157110472 - VBaleha,
re-design and manipulation by Steven C. Schreiner
—Page 3: original graphics: Vecteezy.com; Pixabay.com,
re-design and manipulation by Steven C. Schreiner
—Page 5: original graphic: Pixabay.com/image #3236819,
re-design and manipulation by Steven C. Schreiner
—Page 7: original graphic: Constructer-Dreamstime Stock
Photos, re-design and manipulation by Steven C. Schreiner
—Page 11: original graphic: Pixabay.com/image #1773140,
re-design and manipulation by Steven C. Schreiner
—Page 13: original graphic: Pixabay.com/image #3353781,
re-design and manipulation by Steven C. Schreiner
—Page 14: original graphics: FreeVector.com; Apollofoto-
Dreamstime Stock Photos,
re-design and manipulation by Steven C. Schreiner
—Page 15: original graphics: FreeVector.com,
re-design and manipulation by Steven C. Schreiner
—Page 17: original graphic: FreeVector.com,
re-design and manipulation by Steven C. Schreiner
—Page 19: original graphic: Pixabay.com/image #3055155/
pixel2013-Silvia & Frank-Germany,
re-design and manipulation by Steven C. Schreiner
—Page 23: original graphic: FreeVector.com
—Page 27: original graphic: FreeVector.com
—Page 29: original graphic: FreeVector.com,
re-design and manipulation by Steven C. Schreiner
—Page 31: original graphics: FreeVector.com/Standing power
woman; Pixabay.com/image #3020667,
re-design and manipulation by Steven C. Schreiner
—Page 33: original graphic: FreeVector.com/vector-ballerina

OTHER PHOTOS/GRAPHICS cont.

—Page 39: original graphic: Pixabay.com/image #1888006, re-design and manipulation by Steven C. Schreiner
—Page 41: original graphic: Pixabay.com/image #1710188,
—Page 44: original graphic: Pixabay.com/image #2022820,
—Page 49: original graphic: FreeVector.com
—Page 57: original graphic: Pixabay.com/rose-931641, re-design and manipulation by Steven C. Schreiner
—Page 58: original graphic: Pixabay.com/image #1828538, re-design and manipulation by Steven C. Schreiner
—Page 59: original graphic: Pixabay.com/image #2868220-superkiki, re-design and manipulation by Steven C. Schreiner
—Page 60: original graphic: Pixabay.com/image #591576, re-design and manipulation by Steven C. Schreiner
—Page 63: original graphic: FreeVector.com
—Page 64: original graphic: FreeVector.com

ABOUT THE AUTHOR

C. Steven Blue, producer, publisher, poet, performer,
retired from a 30-year career in stage production in Hollywood, California, now lives with his wife in Eugene, Oregon, where he pursues his passion for poetry, music and the arts.
—As CEO of The Eugene Poetry Foundation, Steven has produced and hosted many poetry, art and music events, including *Open Air In The Square*, Kesey Square (2012); *The Eugene Poetry Open Mic*, New Zone Gallery (2012); *The Poetry Workshop & Poetry Showcase*, Eugene Public Library, as part of the Summer Reading Series (2012-2014); *The Poetry Stage @ Festival of Eugene* (2014-2015); *Burnin' Down The Barnes*, a monthly literary event at the Eugene Barnes & Noble Bookstore (2016-ongoing).
—As publisher and managing Editor of Arrowcloud Press, Steven has published seven books of his own work and three books for others, including the poetry anthologies, *Eugene 150th Birthday Celebration Poetry Collection* - Part of the Eugene, Oregon Sesquicentennial celebration (2012); *Cascadia* - Oregon Student Poetry Contest Anthology of Prize Winning Poems, for the Oregon Poetry Association (2013).
—As poet and performer, Steven has performed his poetry from coast to coast in his unique performance style, using music and hand drums to enhance his readings. His work is published in 12 countries and appears in numerous literary journals and anthologies, both in print and online. He has been interviewed on television and radio and in literary magazines.

65

CONTACT INFORMATION

C. Steven Blue
Producer/Publisher/Poet/Performer

Producer/CEO: The Eugene Poetry Foundation
Publisher/Managing Editor: Arrowcloud Press
Poet/Performer: Available for reading/performing

Website: www.wordsongs.com
Email: cstevenblue@wordsongs.com
Blog: www.wordsongs.com/blog
Facebook author page:
www.facebook.com/cstevenbluepoet
Amazon author page:
www.amazon.com/author/cstevenblue
Twitter: C. Steven Blue
Instagram: cstevenblue
YouTube: C. Steven Blue
Soundcloud: https://soundcloud.com/cstevenblue

Pioneering author of the very first poetry chapbook
published as a Facebook page:
www.facebook.com/591180474377593

OTHER BOOKS BY C. STEVEN BLUE:

WORDSONGS

WILDWEED

Black Tights — Poetry X

S.O.S. ~ Songs Of Sobriety ~
A Personal Journey Of Recovery

The WORDSONGS Series:
Wordsongs (book 1)
Wordsongs—*Too Blue* (book 2)
Wordsongs-3, Recovery (book 3)

OTHER BOOKS PUBLISHED BY ARROWCLOUD PRESS

Eugene 150th Birthday Celebration Poetry Collection

Cascadia #15

songs of the worm whisperer
by karen a. dalyea

Published by

ARROWCLOUD
PRESS

For more information go to www.wordsongs.com

* 9 7 8 0 9 6 3 5 4 9 9 8 3 *